How To Find Your Talents And Strengths

I0482296

HTeBooks

Copyright © 2016

Disclaimer

This book is designed to provide condensed information. It is not intended to reprint all the information that is otherwise available, but instead to complement, amplify and supplement other texts. You are urged to read all the available material, learn as much as possible and tailor the information to your individual needs.

Every effort has been made to make this book as complete and as accurate as possible. However, there may be mistakes, both typographical and in content. Therefore, this text should be used only as a general guide and not as the ultimate source of information. The purpose of this book is to educate.

The author or the publisher shall have neither liability nor responsibility to any person or entity with respect to any loss or damage caused, or alleged to have been caused, directly or indirectly, by the information contained in this book.

Table of Contents

How Will This Book Help You?

"How to Find Your Talents: Simple Ideas for Finding Your Talents and Strengths" is a simple compendium that is written to help out individuals who have not found out their talents and gifts yet.

The tips presented here are very simple to follow and the simplicity of the suggestions will give you more motivation. You will not have any excuses not to follow the tips presented here.

This collection presents ten chapters reinforced with examples and key points.

Enjoy reading this book! Show the world your talent soon.

Know Yourself

"A human being has so many skins inside, covering the depths of the heart. We know so many things, but we don't know ourselves! Why, thirty or forty skins or hides, as thick and hard as an ox's or bear's, cover the soul. Go into your own ground and learn to know yourself there."

– Meister Eckhart

It is easy to find your true talent when you know who you are. By knowing what lies within, you will know ultimately what you want. This is the major requisite for achieving fulfillment and true happiness.

If the experiences you face and the things that you do are all aligned to the things that you truly want, there is a higher probability for you to attract elements into your life that will make you happy. Experts say that this is the key towards having a truly meaningful life. In essence, in order to find your talent, you have to work less and live more.

But are there activities that will actually help you in the process of knowing yourself better? Actually there are lots of them. Here are some activities highly recommended by experts:

Do some meditation

Regular meditation is the key towards quieting your mind. When you're successful in quieting your mind, you can enjoy inner peace, balance, and true joy. This is the major condition required for acquiring more knowledge. This way, you can be more open with less judgment involved.

Expose your core values

Observe how you react to situations and find the time to analyze what your core values are. Every once in a while, do some introspection or reflection to examine and analyze your own values. That way, you will not only find your true interests, you will find more reasons live the next days to the fullest. Instead of dwelling on other people's expectations, why not try to make a set of your own. When you finally figure out what you truly want to do, then you will be able to plan accordingly what you will do without deviating from the top values that you have.

Stop expecting too much

Be more spontaneous because expectations can somewhat alter your direction. It can block you from discovering your talents, so never set the bar too high to the point of your forgetting who you truly are. Once you learn the art of letting go of your expectations, you will see that it is so much easier to be your true self regardless of the situation that you are facing. Examine each of your expectation. Let go of those which you think are disproportionate for you.

Let go of relationships that are by nature, conditional

At this point, let go of other people's expectations. Stop busying yourself with living another person's life by following what others are saying. Unconditional relationships are meant to nurture you with support and not torture you with unreasonable expectations.

Care for yourself and watch your back

Connect with your talents and your true self by doing activities that makes you feel good, fulfilled, and relaxed. It can be any of the following: take a gym class, go to bed early, or read a favorite book. If you have moments of relaxation every once in a while, you will be better oriented to know yourself.

The road towards discovering your true talent begins with knowing yourself from deep within.

Stop Making Excuses

"No excuses and no sob stories. Life is full of excuses if you're looking. I have no time to gripe over misfortune. I don't waste time looking back."

– Junior Seau

Use your gifts, they always say. But there are many of us who keep on believing that we do not have any. If you are stuck with that kind of excuse, there is a great chance that the world will not ever see what you are great at. It is kind of shocking and frustrating finding too many people who dwell on excuses instead of being more proactive.

But we should look at models. There are many successful people around us who could have dwelt on unreasonable excuses. If Zuckerberg, for example, made an excuse that he's just a college undergrad, perhaps we will not have Facebook today. If Obama was overcome by the excuses made by other people for him, then he won't be a two-term US president.

If you will choose to make excuses, you won't discover your gift. Without discovering your inner talent or gift, living life to the fullest will not even be possible. Time is ticking constantly. Before you know it, you might have wasted a lot of time already. Before falling into a situation wherein you no longer have any other option but regret, why not pursue your gifts instead?

Never be afraid of making new discoveries about yourself. It would not entail that much of a threat to the status quo. Many people fall into this absurd belief that discovering your talents would involve making big and radical changes in your life. That is not true. There's no reason for you to think that way.

Here are some steps for you to discover your talents and say no to excuses:

First, you need to open your eyes and wake up to the reality. Give yourself that much-needed wake up call. Whenever you say that you do not have any gifts or talents, just remind yourself that it is not true. Everyone is born with a certain gift or talent that may be unique. It is just that we keep on ignoring our own gifts. Here's what you have to do: keep your heart and mind open. List down what you love to do. Also, take notice of the activities that you find pleasure doing. Think of it this way: talents do not really have to be grandiose, spectacular, or larger-than-life.

Everyone begins with something small. A talent can grow or vanish depending on how you choose nurture it. There are clues that can lead to the eventual discovery of your talents. You can get help from other people. Note that there is a separate chapter meant for discussing how listening to other people's opinions about your skills can lead to the discovery of your talents and gifts.

Aside from other people, listen to the voice from within. You have to trust what your inner self is saying. Listen to your personal intuition and be personally surprised by how accurate your inner voice is. There are other people who call the inner voice a "gut feeling."

Know why you are driven to find your talent. You must have a reason, and you should be very vocal about it. Remind yourself every single day of why you are trying to look for your talent. Are you trying to pursue a higher level of satisfaction? Are you trying to dodge potential sources of pain? Are you trying to relieve some sort of displeasure?

By not making excuses, you will be more open to discoveries. You will know what really motivates you, and at the same time, you will know what kills your spirit.

Try to craft an appropriate response to the question: "What drives you in finding your talent or your gift?" A good response would be, aside from being realistic, is a response that can lift your morale and assist in picking up your momentum. Do you want to experience something better? Do you want to have a higher level of vigor? Would you want to have more enthusiasm? Visualize the answers and firmly set it inside your head. Your answers to these questions

will give you an extra push, and it will take you a few steps further each time.

Once you have become aware of your special gifts and talents and the reasons behind each, your mind—both the unconscious and the unconscious—will give you more bits of evidence that will finally cement your firm belief in yourself. Keep on searching, answer the difficult questions including those that are led by "why," and say no to all the excuses that are playing around your head. Never give in to excuses.

Never give in to any of those excuses that are running in your head. It is just a mechanism of your mind to make things easier for you. But these will only hinder your growth as a person and your discovery of your gifts.

Do a Bit of Self-Affirmation

"Affirmations are our mental vitamins, providing the
supplementary positive thoughts we need to balance the barrage
of negative events and thoughts we experience daily."
— Tia Walker, The Inspired Caregiver: Finding Joy While Caring
for Those You Love

It might be considered as a cliché, but it rings true: you truly are what you think. From an idealists' point of view, the events in our lives are actually deeply rooted from our very thoughts. But from a realist's point of view, life is not only about thoughts. We should do something to translate them into words, and the words should be converted into actions that represent what is inside our head and in our heart.

In finding your true talent and gifts, you need to be careful in choosing your words. You need to choose to say only the things that will be working towards your personal benefit. This way, you will be able to cultivate and nourish your highest personal good. This can be done by doing self-affirmations. They can be very helpful in the process of purification of thoughts and in the restructuring the brain dynamics. If you psych yourself that nothing is truly impossible, you can achieve anything. Meaning to say, it will not be impossible for you to discover your inner gifts and your hidden talents.

By virtue of etymology, the word affirmation comes from the Latin word *affirmare*, which means to strengthen or to make steady. So, in the literal sense, affirmation is the process of steadying yourself. Psychologists say that affirmations increase your chance of harnessing your potentials. But how exactly are you going to do the affirmation process?

First, you have to believe that you possess a certain talent, gift, or potential. Then, you have to do the affirmation verbally. Verbalize your ambitions and dreams and say it clearly to yourself. By doing this, you will instantly refuel and empower yourself via reassurance.

The wishful thinking—that you will be able to find your talents—can then turn into reality.

Self-improvement and self-discovery can truly occur through self-affirmation. In fact, neuropsychologists have conducted studies that will prove that such affirmations can result to physiological change. In fact, the physiological change occurs in the brain through the process of rewiring. This is very similar to exercise because it can increase the level of hormones that make you feel better about yourself. The effect of such hormones is the upsurge of positivity and happy thoughts transmitted in your neurons. Additionally, it has been established that affirmations are very important in the avoidance of negative speech, negative thoughts and their manifestation, which are negative actions.

In shaping our future, and in the process of knowing ourselves better and unraveling our capabilities, it is always important to master the art of verbalizing our thoughts. Spiritual advisers are very consistent in saying that the universe can be influenced by each word that we utter. The art that we should master is the art of dictating our wishes. Believe it or not, the universe truly responds.

Here are some affirmations that prove to be helpful in unraveling your talents:

(*) I am my own life's architect, and I have the capability to strengthen its foundation and select the contents.

(*) The energy that I have now is overflowing, and it translates to true joy.

(*) I am perfectly happy. I have a brilliant mind. I have a tranquil spirit.

(*) No amount of negative thoughts or low points can put me down.

(*) I have endless talents. I will begin using them all today.

(*) Those who harmed me in the past, I forgive them all now. I detach from them and the pains they caused me peacefully.

(*) I have a lot of compassion from deep within, and it will not allow me to dwell on anger again because I have a lot of love to give.

(*) I have what it takes to be truly successful.

(*) My endeavors are all leading to success.

(*) My mind is brimming with creative ideas.

(*) I choose to be happy because I have a lot of blessings and accomplishments.

(*) I have the unlimited capability to overcome any challenge. My chance to being successful someday is infinite.

(*) I choose to stand by my decisions because they will help me succeed.

(*) I will prosper because I choose to be positive. Life has a lot more to offer.

(*) I choose to detach myself from negative habits and create new and positive ones.

(*) Many people know that I am worthy of their respect and admiration.

(*) I have a family that supports me every step of the way and my friends are equally wonderful.

(*) I have a high level of confidence because I know what I am truly worth.

(*) The things that I am dealing with now are mere preparation for something that is really good.

(*) No one can destroy me. No amount of distractions can break me.

(*) Pain is temporary, glory is forever.

(*) I plan today to have the perfect kind of tomorrow.

(*) The universe will allow me to find my true talents. My dreams will soon become a reality.

(*) I was born to be a great person. No obstacles or difficulty can stop me.

(*) I always function with a clear mind. I decide with a pure heart.

(*) All my fears and hesitations are slowly but surely disappearing.

These affirmations can be utilized in order to find your strengths and locate your talents and gifts. With these, you will better communicate with the universe and invite positive energy. Dreams and aspirations do become a reality.

Listen to Others

"This is the problem with dealing with someone who is actually a good listener. They don't jump in on your sentences, saving you from actually finishing them, or talk over you, allowing what you do manage to get out to be lost or altered in transit. Instead, they wait, so you have to keep going."

— Sarah Dessen, Just Listen

Listening, in itself, is a gift. Not everyone gets to master it because not everyone realizes its true worth. But if you can be a great listener, you will have a better idea of what's really happening around you. You will also see yourself in a much better light if you will listen to what other people are saying.

If you aspire to find your true talent and aspirations, you need to find a good leader, coach, and facilitator. And you should listen to what they have to say.

If you will choose to listen, you will build that sense of trust. Other people will trust you and your talent, and you will begin to trust in yourself if you will learn how to listen. In the process of listening to what others have to say, you can change your perspective and decide to make things a bit better.

If you learn how to listen, you will find out other people's justification behind the talents, skills, and gifts that they see in you. Also, the more you listen sincerely, the more credible you will appear to be. If you are credible, it will be much easier for them to believe in your skills and talents. It will be easier for you to reach your dreams.

Furthermore, if you will learn how to listen properly, you will find out that there are people who can appreciate your worth. By showing that you know how to listen, other people will show a greater degree of support and concern to you. In the process of listening, you will not only discover your talent, you will also show people that you respect them and that they are important to you.

In addition, listening can help you get things and tasks done. By actively listening, you can better identify and set goals.

By listening, you can acquire all sorts of information. Note however, that some of the information that you will acquire may not be among those that you need. Some are very useful while some are worth keeping. Either way, keep your ears, mind, and heart open.

Finally, listening helps open the idea of exchange. If you are in the process of unraveling your talent, then listen on how you can further improve what you already have. This way, you will be a step closer to your goals.

Keep your ears, heart, and mind open. You will be surprised by how much you will learn about yourself and your talent by simply listening.

Understand and Practice the Art of Solitude

"We must become so alone, so utterly alone, that we withdraw into our innermost self. It is a way of bitter suffering. But then our solitude is overcome, we are no longer alone, for we find that our innermost self is the spirit, that it is God, the indivisible. And suddenly we find ourselves in the midst of the world, yet undisturbed by its multiplicity, for our innermost soul we know ourselves to be one with all being."

— Hermann Hesse

Having some time alone is essential in the process of self-discovery because it helps you in better connecting with your inner self.

Experts say that if you want to know your talent, you need to spend a significant amount of your time alone. But the sad thing is that solitude can now be truly considered as among the lost arts. Truth be told, solitude is usually correlated with antisocial tendency of individuals. People who dwell in antisocial behaviors are oftentimes misjudged as being soaked in sadness and loneliness.

But don't fall into such hasty generalizations. Solitude cannot be equated to sadness. Instead, it is a healthy mechanism wherein you can derive quite a number of psychological and physical benefits.

So, what exactly are the benefits of solitude?

Solitude gives you the chance to relax a bit and have a fresher line of thought; you can better unwind with the help of solitude because the brain will be able to take a good rest and replenish itself. Not having any companion around means that you have no distractions to deal with and you can clear your thoughts. That way, you can better think and focus.

Solitude helps in uncovering your talent because it improves productivity and increases the level of concentration. By concentrating well, all of the interruptions and distractions will be effectively removed. You can now focus on your quest to find out what sort of talent or gift lies within.

Solitude gives you the chance to hear your inner voice and better discover yourself. If you are always with other people, you will tend to neglect what you truly want to say. Your opinion will most likely be ignored, and your desires will not be considered really important. Other people's voices tend to "drown" your inner voice. Never let that happen. Try solitude.

Solitude buys you the much needed time to do an in-depth thinking. The things that you have to do on a day-to-day basis seem to have no ending. In order to momentarily free yourself from such, you must first take some time alone to think of things that are important to you. That way, you will be able to enhance your creativity.

Solitude is beneficial because it enhances your skill in solving problems in a more effective manner. By taking some time alone, you will be able to free yourself from distractions.

Your relationship with other people is more likely to be enhanced if you experience solitude every once in a while. If you spend some time with yourself on a regular basis, you can better understand what you want to achieve and what sort of dreams you wish to realize someday. Solitude also helps you make choices that are better aligned with your goals. You can better appreciate the talents that you already have if you are experiencing solitude.

In case you are wondering how exactly you can spend time in solitude, here are some techniques that you might find useful.

Disconnect with the world

Solitude can be a bit challenging to achieve because of the prevalence of gadgets and other forms of technology. So in order to do this effectively, disconnect. Turn off your Android phone and disconnect from the Internet. Unplug your television.

Go to the workplace one to two hours earlier than the usual

That way, you can be sure that there is no one yet in the workplace. You can buy time for yourself to meditate and spend some quiet time alone.

Do not leave your room and lock your door

This is the simplest option that you can take. No need to go somewhere far away. Just lock the door, put a sign and make the world understand that you are spending this time alone.

Try to eat your lunch alone

As a rule, never eat at your work desk. While it is a good time to catch up with friends, it is an equally good opportunity for you to catch up with yourself. You do not have to eat your lunch alone every single day. Doing this option at least once a week is more than enough.

Put the "me time" on schedule

If you are keeping a planner, make sure that you literally mark the date for the scheduled solitude so that you can spend time discovering your talents and potentials. Just like any other activity, if you are not going to put it on schedule, you will have this tendency of leaving it out.

Spending some time alone is perfect for knowing what lies within your mind and heart. It is also good for uncovering your hidden talents. Solitude is definitely not for the lonely. It is for the curious.

Recognize and Develop Your Talent

"There is a fountain of youth: it is your mind, your talents, the creativity you bring to your life and the lives of people you love. When you learn to tap this source, you will truly have defeated age."

– Sophia Loren

You are probably aware of your basic skills. More than anyone else, you can tell what you can and what you cannot do. And these basic skills are usually the starting point of truly extraordinary talents. But it begins with recognizing the existence of the skill so that you can do something to develop and work on it further.

Many people do not get to maximize their skills and reach the full realization of their talents because they chose to ignore what they already have. For example, if you are sensitive to melodies and tunes, do not ignore your skill and capabilities connected to it. Try to sing more. Join a choir. Select a voice coach who can monitor your progress. A lot of talents have been lost because of the owners' decisions to ignore what they have.

Time and again, it has been proven that it is always easier to recognize other people's talents and ignore your own. We often compare what we have to what others have, but that should not be the case. You are unique and your skill set is never identical with that of others. There might be some sort of resemblance, but no two skill sets and talents are identical.

It all begins with discovering and recognizing your talent. Be sure to search your personal, artistic, and creative abilities. Enumerate the activities that you wish to be engaged in. By making this list, you will be able to point out your talents and you can begin enhancing them.

The next step is doing something to actively develop your talent. Talents take a great deal of effort and time to develop, so you should be serious about this feat. If you can remember the time when you are trying to learn walking, writing, and reading, it can be as tedious as that. Others compare developing an existing talent with learning a new language. It takes some serious and conscious effort. You should recognize the fact that perhaps you need to spend some time practicing and rehearsing.

Of course it can be tedious, tiring, and exhausting. A lot of people have already given up on developing or honing their talents. They end up regretting that they did not pursue their talents because they found themselves in a situation wherein they needed it.

On the other hand, there are a lot of people who are thankful for honing their talents in the past despite the difficulty they faced in the past. It pays off to discover, recognize, and develop your talent.

Talents are very much like problems. Unless you recognize their existence, you won't be able to do something about it.

Believe in What You Can Do

"Believe in yourself, and the rest will fall into place. Have faith in your own abilities, work hard, and there is nothing you cannot accomplish."

– Brad Henry

You are a unique being. As a special individual, you need to recognize the fact that the world will not be complete unless you share your talent and capability. Believe in your potentials and in what you can actually do. Never say "I can't" because it can only invite negativity. Whenever you feel bad, ask people who care and those who are ready to provide you with the necessary support.

If you feel that you cannot do it anymore, just tell yourself: "This too shall pass." Whenever you feel like saying: "I've reached my limit," just remember that your potentials are limitless. Aspire to either maintain or improve. Just do not stop. Strive to be better every single time.

Again, it is important to listen to criticisms and take them constructively. Of course, not all opinions about you and your talent will be positive. Sometimes, they can be disheartening if you will take them the wrong way. No matter what other people say, try to aspire for improvement. That is the only way to go. Never lose your passion and face the challenges with courage.

Finally, you need to learn all the necessary skills to make your talent extraordinary. Study what it takes to be better and to develop your talent. You may read several resource materials like books. Also, you can ask people who are willing to be your critic or mentor. Watch movies and take lessons that will enhance your world view. Never be afraid to do your best.

If ever you make mistakes, never give up. The mistakes will only teach you and assist you in making your talents better.

Believe in your talent. Be the first to have faith. And never give up. Strive to be the best.

Give Everything Else a Try

"All growth is a leap in the dark, a spontaneous unpremeditated act without benefit of experience."

– Henry Miller

Be a natural. Never be afraid to spontaneously show your talents. Feel free to sing, dance, play any instrument, paint, rap, or act. Keep your hand full—literally and figuratively. If you can play any sport—be it indoor or outdoor—do not hesitate to play. Do what you can do with one hundred percent passion.

You may find yourself to be a mediocre in things that you do for the first time, but there are only a handful who can do thing perfectly in their first try. Give every single talent a try because it is the only way that you can discover what you can do and what you cannot do. Keep a journal or a record to take note of the things that you can be potentially good in. Take note of the ones that you are comfortable doing. If you are not good in something, be extra honest to admit it so that you will not be wasting time doing it.

In a lot of instances in our life, we tend to tell ourselves that we can't do something. Technically, it is alright to come up with such a conclusion if you have already tried. But the biggest mistake here is if you give up even without trying. It is analogous to putting up that white flag even before you meet your actual enemy.

Be open to surprises. The best times in a person's life are usually when he or she surprises themselves. Once you experience this, you will find something interesting in yourself again.

If you haven't tried rock climbing yet, try it. If you have not tried scuba diving, give it a go. If you haven't tried writing a book, ask someone who can. Put up a business. Start small. Never be afraid to fail. Even failures present important lessons.

It might be helpful to take into consideration the things that you already know. What are your skills? What can you do? From these bits of information, you have a clue on what is the best thing that you should do.

There is no harm in trying. Never give up unless you have already given a good fight.

Step out of Your Comfort Zone

"I want to challenge you today to get out of your comfort zone. You have so much incredible potential on the inside. God has put gifts and talents in you that you probably don't know anything about."

– Joel Osteen

While providing you comfort, the comfort zone can be some sort of labyrinth that can limit what you can do. There are a lot of people who get stuck in their comfort zone and they end up not trying anything new.

By choosing to stay inside your comfort zone, you deny yourself of all forms of changes. You say no to negative changes, but you also forego the positive one. By staying inside that circle of comfort, you do not give yourself a chance to spend some effort and time to aspire for what you dream and aspire for.

Why is this the case then? Simple—because it is uncomfortable to step out of the comfort zone. And you can't blame yourself for being too afraid of the unknown and the uncertain.

Is there a shortcut towards luring yourself out of the comfort zone? There are simple techniques, but these usually take time. Here are some of the steps that you can take:

Mix up the small things and surprise yourself as often as possible.

For example, when it comes to music, never stick to a single genre. Try new kinds of music. Download tunes that you haven't tried before. See if you will enjoy it. The same goes with food. Pick something from the menu that you have not tried before. When you buy books, try a title that does not fit your personality well. Finally, when you are going home, try a path that you haven't tried before.

By doing these, you will most likely try to develop a talent that you never thought that you have before.

Take it one step at a time.

Never rush. Facing changes can be very difficult. It can be scary to make the big shift. The result is to procrastinate. With that, no positive changes can be expected. In order for you to step out of your comfort zone, try to take really small steps towards your goal. You do not have to be in a hurry. Sometimes, it is better to get there slowly.

Never do it alone.

It is best to step out of the comfort zone if you know that you are not alone. If you have a friend who also wishes to discover his hidden talents, encourage him to join you in your quest towards self-discovery. It is always easier to go somewhere if you know if you have company.

The comfort zone can only provide you comfort, nothing more and nothing less. If you want to experience something new and exciting in your life, try to step out of it. Your extraordinary skills and talents can only be found if you choose to ignore your comfort for once. It is going to be truly worth it.

Practice and Develop Your Talent

"Use what talents you possess; the woods would be very silent if no birds sang there except those that sang best."

– Henry Van Dyke

Practice is the only key towards perfection. Many basketball superstars once found themselves imperfect or mediocre in their craft. They chose to spend time and effort to practice and develop their skills.

Practice is the only way for you to control your talent. You can only experience progress if you are determined in developing your gift. A lot of skills that are necessary for perfecting a talent require a lot of repetition. Yes, it can take a few hours, several days, numerous weeks, or even years before you can truly say that you are ready to show the world your talent.

For once in our life, we have already shown the pure determination. If you find yourself talking or walking right now, it is because of the fact that you had the determination to learn when you were a toddler. If you can only use that level of determination and will power in every single endeavor that you are involved in, no talent is impossible to perfect.

At the end of the day, do not complain. Just do something to be better, and you will be surprised at the result.

Once you are done with this, you are ready to show the world your talent. When you are ready, never hide it. Pick an audience and sing, dance, or ask them to listen. A talent is worthless unless it is shared. The joy that it can cause others can never be paralleled.

Practice is the only key towards perfection. Never lose that passion. Keep on trying.

How to Apply Key Ideas for the Best Results?

This compendium discusses several techniques for you to discover your talent. Now, it is up to you to put these tips into action.

Your talents will remain hidden unless you do something about it. Show the world what you can do and you will be surprised with the amount of joy that you will be able to share. Not to mention the happiness that you will feel due to the sense of fulfillment.

www.ingramcontent.com/pod-product-compliance
Lightning Source LLC
Chambersburg PA
CBHW070425190526
45169CB00003B/1411